FREE TO BE

Shake Doubt, Discover You

MAUREEN THOMAS

FREE TO BE. Copyright © 2021. Maureen Thomas. All Rights Reserved.

No portion of this book may be reproduced, stored in a retrieval system, or transmitted in any form or by any means, except for brief quotations in printed reviews, without the prior written permission of DayeLight Publishers or Maureen Thomas.

Published by

DAYELight
PUBLISHERS

ISBN: 978-1-953759-42-9 (paperback)

Scripture quotations marked "KJV" are taken from the Holy Bible, King James Version (Public Domain).

This book is dedicated to my grandmother, Albertha "Sissy" Benjamin, who allowed me to see faith, favor, and blessings in action. Though challenged by reading, she was never defeated by life.

Acknowledgments

I am absolutely grateful to my God and Savior, who has kept me thus far, and I continue to press in fortitude for purpose and a full life.

To my wonderful parents, Monica and Sylvester Thomas, I love and appreciate you beyond measure, and it filled my heart to hear you both ask, "When will this book be completed so I can hold it in my hand." Those words alone have completed me.

To my brother, friend, pastor, and leader, Apostle Jeremiah, your tenacity for me not to abide in the shadows goes without reservation. May you continue to be the beacon of light that shines and prepares the pathway for others to follow.

Kareen, my sister-in-law, your quiet support has been felt throughout this entire journey.

To Apostle Cherry, who has been my mentor, father, and standard keeper; I am thankful for the day you walked into my life. I often wonder where I would be, and it is not a thought worth exploring. May continuous honor, favor, and blessings by God's divine outpouring continue to overflow in your life as the prolific teacher I know you to be.

To Evangelist McKnight and Elder Darrion, who prayed for me throughout this entire process; thank you for being my warriors and gatekeepers and for staying with me until the very end.

Last but certainly not least, to the two persons who hold a very special place in my heart, Minister Andrea Midgette and Elder Lorenzo Blair; you championed me to read each chapter line by line and precepts upon precepts. You never held back when something worked and when it required me to push even deeper. Your unwavering support pushed me even when I thought I had no more to give. I will be forever indebted to your unrestrained honesty and support, and for that I can declare, "NO WAY COULD I HAVE DONE THIS WITHOUT YOU and YOU!" From the bottom of my heart, I declare an overflow of blessings over you both for a debt of gratitude I can never repay.

To all my family and friends who have just said yes, go ahead and get this done; gratefulness is the portion that I give back to you.

Table of Contents

Acknowledgments v
Introduction 9
Chapter 1 When You Sleep On Your Sofa, Only To Find Out You Are Lost 11
Chapter 2 Finding The Me Within Me! Opening The Door To Change 17
Chapter 3 Forgive And Forget - How Do I Do That? 27
Chapter 4 Words Have Power – You Have Power With Your Words 43
Chapter 5 Laugh At Yourself A Lot – Going Through The Waves .. 57
Chapter 6 Dream A Little – It Will Take You Somewhere 65
Chapter 7 Own You 75
Chapter 8 Ask, Seek, Knock 91
About the Author 99

Introduction

We can either become shadows of ourselves or decide to live our best lives by embracing obstacles, change, and pursuing new avenues to maturity. Have you ever known deep down inside that you were not living up to your fullest potential, and yet you could not seem to get a break on how to get moving? This was my issue for a long time.

I chose to write this book so I can share my journey of becoming a better person than I was yesterday. This is not a "Cinderella" story with a perfect ending; it is a conversation from me to you that will allow you to laugh at yourself, forgive yourself and, most importantly, love yourself in order to get up and keep going. There is greatness in you to be offered to this world. Seize the opportunity to rediscover the zeal and joy that is lying dormant inside of you and make a decision to get up and start again. Wherever you have found yourself with the pause button on your life, this is an encouraging message for you to change your situation like yesterday's shirt and put on a new attitude of embracing the new.

"Some people come into your life as blessings; some come in your life as lessons." – Mother Theresa.

Chapter 1

When You Sleep On Your Sofa, Only To Find Out You Are Lost

One night you made a pit stop on the sofa, with the television lined up in front of it, and you woke up the next day with the television watching you. But then, the one night pit stop became a habit, and sleeping on your sofa with the television babysitting you became a permanent place. One day the question came, "Why am I here?"

Personal Testimony

I started this habit and realized I did not know when I started feeling afraid to sleep in my own bed. On the sofa, I controlled whatever was looming out there trying to get me. On the sofa, I could stop thinking, stop processing and just stay in a perpetual freeze zone, with the television as my anchor into someone else's reality. There was this need to keep whatever was plaguing me at bay.

Free To Be

I had created the perfect space for my beautiful, spacious bedroom; no television, enough room to walk around my bed, nice wood floor with an area rug, large windows left partially open to allow a light breeze to gently blow my beautiful floor length curtains, yet peaceful sleep eluded me when it was time to go to this "tranquil" space.

One night, while lying on the sofa, I had a dream that someone entered my apartment, and we had a struggle. While we were wrestling, I was standing outside my door, and the intruder was on the inside.

I woke up so frightened and scared that I began to question the very meaning of the dream. It continued to plague me until I realized that I had allowed an intruder into my mind and spirit, and I was dying.

Becoming Honest With Myself

The revelation came that my conscience was pushing through my dreams in order for me to stop hiding and to stop dying. My destiny and purpose were dying, and they were trying to get my attention by any means necessary. In that moment, I noticed that although I was breathing and functioning, I was simply existing. Life's disappointments had taken its toll on me, and I had become a robot in the habits of life. Over time, I had built a fortress around myself that even I needed a passcode to get in.

- Are you dangerous?

- Are you going to take it all and disappear?
- Is this smile genuine?
- What do you really want?

These quandaries ran around in my head and kept me busy from facing my true self. Was I a coward for not taking a chance on anything? Yet, the question remained, "How did I get here?"

The moment I had to sleep with the lights on was when people-pleasing or trying to be perfect came into play, creating a sense of hypocrisy against my own self. Afraid of being who I really am, knowing I had inner strength, yet completely terrified of turning on the lights that brings revelation to my life on full blast.

Take A Step And Take A Chance

I decided to release myself from the traps in my mind; traps which seemed to protect me from danger actually prevented me from experiencing life. I reminded myself that there is a time for *everything under the sun; a time to laugh and a time to cry, a time to live and a time to die. (See Ecclesiastes 3:4).* I went through a valley period where I questioned my self-worth and discovered that I kept the external lights on because I did not know how to allow my inner light to shine.

I began to claim good things for myself. There are moments when we see the full potential of others. We may even see the path they should take, and the vision is so clear. However, when it comes to one's own life, the view is a bit foggy. If I am to believe that

Free To Be

everything here is for a set purpose, then I must also believe that I am part of the whole, and somehow I am blocking and obscuring my own vision.

I sat back one day and considered my future that had become sketchy at best.

Reflection: I had a job, but while I liked the people and what I did, there was something quite unfulfilled in me. Feeling unaccomplished is a very disappointing way to live one's life, and it ate away at me from the inside. Even as I discovered that I was simply existing and not living, I found it difficult to jump-start my life. Every day is a gift to begin afresh and start something new. I was either going to exist in disappointments or investigate and identify the real me.

One day, someone had to hold my hand and ask, "Can you see it?" I was confused, so he continued, "Look out there at your life and see the people you are holding hostage or in bondage because you have locked yourself away from the world."

For a moment, it was easy to think that "crazy" was talking to me. However, I took that moment to tap into the truth that I was hiding and living in a shell that was just blending and going with the "flow."

Being trapped in my own body and wanting to emerge, I looked up and looked as far as I could possibly imagine, and it was like a movie screen appeared before me. I was not Oprah or anyone else; I was just me. I was not wearing a cape like a superhero or holding a magic wand; it was just me:

- Laughing out loud
- Ministering
- Crying
- Challenging myself to be better
- Cruising on a yacht
- Flying in a private jet
- Walking along the beach
- Owning my own business
- Helping others
- Speaking before an audience
- Having a loving family
- Dancing

The joy of the Lord is my strength! (See Nehemiah 8:10). With this knowledge, I was being challenged to be free, and I had to do something about it. I had to find out why I placed myself in a shell and then release myself from the things that have kept me there.

I needed to face the monsters and the dragons of my imagination and free myself in order to truly declare that, *"I can do all things through Christ who strengthens me!" (See Philippians 4:13).*

I will give you sweet sleep, says the Lord. (See Proverbs 3:24). When I was younger, I loved to sleep in complete darkness. If the room was not dark enough, I would throw my blanket over my head to seal the deal.

I went back to my bedroom, to the comfort of my bed. There was no television in my room, so I was back to embracing the darkness of precious sleep there, and behind my eyelids, I could see all of me. There was no better feeling than acknowledging and accepting that I am like no other and there is no one else like me. Going back to my own bed again, I allowed sweet sleep to take over.

The sofa is for entertainment.

Go back to bed.

At this point, I allowed myself to go free!

Ask "How do I get past here?"

Seek the ways to get moving again.

Knock out the thoughts that placed you in shackles.

Join me in the process of taking control of your own life so you too can truly shout from the inside out: ***"I am free to be!"***

Chapter 2

Finding The Me Within Me! Opening The Door To Change

I made a conscious decision to investigate the matter of the "me" within myself who wanted to be different, dramatic, new, and revealed as transformed. The "me" within had the curiosity of a baby: ready to observe the wonders of the world for the first time in all its splendor and beauty, touching and exploring new places and things. As I thought about this, I decided to sit up straighter and challenge myself to pull the newness out of me. I discovered there was a shout echoing from my belly – "LET ME OUT!"

A fountain of gifts and talents resides inside each of us and is waiting to be discovered. We can become our own worst enemy when we have the belief that "it is not possible" or "it is unachievable." At some point in our lives, we have all sought to determine if there is more awaiting us. This door to the "me" that needed to be released was based on this one decision: *"Will I go all the way?"*

Opening the door to the new you will require changes and breaking habits of sliding back into familiar patterns, which can lead to a repeat of cycles that no longer benefit your life; patterns that will not reflect the changes that you desire and crave to explore and those that have defined you.

Excuses will always arise and provide reasonable arguments to convince you that it is quite okay to do absolutely nothing about discovering the new you that is waiting to emerge. However, the new you will always be knocking on the door of your heart with a desire to be released. If you are listening intently, you will hear yourself asking, "Will I be given the opportunity, care, fortitude, attention, and nourishment to grow?"

Personal Story

I lived a fairly decent life while growing up. There was no silver spoon in my mouth; however, my childhood lacked nothing. My needs were met, and I have very nostalgic teenage years that I cherish. My family was considered as hardworking individuals, and I learned by experience to become a responsible adult by having a good education, a job that can sustain my lifestyle, and being an upstanding member of society. Fostering my dreams, which were many at the time, was never cultivated. Therefore, the prospects of fulfilling my given talent or gifts were never a topic for discussion. So I never fully realized what dreams could have been accomplished had I received proper mentorship. Being bright, smart, and capable of pushing into any area of interest without being mentored led me to lead a "safe" life without really stretching into anything adventurous.

Living a good life for me meant being able to travel and enjoy my friends and family. However, I discovered that something was missing on the inside, even though I was exhibiting quite the opposite on the outside. On the outside, I appeared all put together, as I was able to maintain a lifestyle that our society deems successful. However, peace eluded me because there was still a birthing that needed to take place, and it began to be more persistent in knocking from the inside.

Apostle Cherry, my spiritual father, grabbed hold of my hand one day and told me to look into the future and take responsibility for my life that I had imprisoned by not venturing outside of my comfort zone. It was confusing and exciting at the same time to discover that there was more for me to offer and a definite purpose and destiny to be fulfilled. Walking around with this sense of wonder that had given me a new lease on life, I began to question how to unlock the mystery of newness in me and, oh boy, what a journey when you venture to open the door.

There must be a conviction to continue through the open door of change, so comfort and stagnation are unable to drown the desire to become the new you. You must go beyond the curiosity that is not only piqued but opens you up to seeking, asking, learning, and embracing newness.

The place to receive victory and freedom from captivity and stagnation is in our minds.

The thoughts we allow to linger in our minds are the ones that stay and become our focus; therefore, manifesting in our lives. So the way we observe and analyze things could cause us to wrestle with questions like:

- What do I have to learn?
- Will I get through all these lessons?
- Am I too old for this?
- What will others think?
- Will people think it is not fair?

All the above materialized, not because we have tried and failed, but because we try to complete them in our minds without moving, speaking, and acting on what we believe.

Are you bold enough to grab hold of the possibilities in your dreams, to take a step, and MOVE?

Stepping into a new area of your life means making a decision to embrace new challenges and openly embracing your acquired knowledge and expertise in different areas of your life; also, allowing yourself to freely admit what you do not know. Both aspects of this truth will better enable you to share your expertise and freely learn new ideas and concepts from a whole new world filled with people who will bring their own creativity and a new perspective into your life. This serves to inspire, create, produce and make a difference that can propel you to fulfill your destiny which is calling out to you from the inside.

The first and hardest step for most of us sometimes is allowing people into a space we hold sacred, not knowing if they will add value with a positive experience or decrease value in what we perceive as a negative experience based on our expectations.

No matter how hard we try to steal ourselves from it, we will never live fully unless we experience people; we can never be whole until we are able to embrace differences and even disappointments in ourselves and others. When we avoid participation and interaction with others, we stunt the process of our own growth. *"Difficulties must be embraced in order to live an extraordinary life."* We must overcome obstacles in order to look from the mountain and declare, "I did it!"

So how can I change? Or why should I change?

Transformation requires you to focus completely on the part of you that needs to emerge. Shifting blame will simply be a cop-out from the reshaping that is taking place from the inside out.

There is a saying, *"We can change no one but ourselves!"* Delving into a new venture often brings discomfort because the territory is new and unfamiliar. Anything new requires us to begin a process of learning and acquiring knowledge on how to proceed. You will get invited into new territories that can bring excitement, which makes you wonder where you have been and what has been holding you back all along. You must do all you can to absorb everything and not become stuck with just a good feeling in these moments. On the flip side of excitement, you can be presented with confusion, bewilderment, or being overwhelmed, which can create resentment in the process of change. This can stir up your emotions and cause you to start shifting blame unto others when there is misunderstanding, suffering, or disagreement. Why does this happen? It happens because the answers or the revelations are not quick enough for your liking.

When you are faced with the challenge of dealing with and controlling your emotions, you can continue pushing ahead. You will not throw in the towel just because your feelings get hurt or someone betrays you. Even if the feelings of inadequacy grab hold of you, there must be a reminder that the breakthrough is at the end of every hurt and struggle. Giving up before the breakthrough will place your life on the precipice of regret.

"I am the true vine, and my Father is the husbandman. Every branch in me that beareth not fruit he taketh away: and every branch that <u>beareth</u> fruit, he purgeth it, that it may bring forth more fruit." (John 15:1-2 - KJV).

This scripture brings a beautiful reminder that the pruning of a tree produces even better fruit. Therefore, better growth requires that pressure be applied to every area of your life that needs adjustments or repair. This will reflect a newness that you can walk in so others may recognize the solid fruit that you are becoming or have become through pruning.

Therefore, the challenge lies in finding out what will complete, satisfy and define you in such a way that you are holding nothing back and always putting out your best effort. Your best might not always be good enough, but you must know that you gave it your best effort. You can begin to see yourself as someone who is no longer standing on the sidelines but someone who has begun to be a full participant in life. Regardless of the low points, celebrate the high ones while not getting stuck in either direction because you have dared to progressively pull on something greater.

You might ask yourself, "Where is the measure for me to perform a self-assessment?" One of the best insights is to check your conscience meter; if you are open to listen, you will always hear.

We are our best selves when we give. It does not matter what is required to be given, deep down on the inside, you know when you have cheated yourself from "giving," and when you do, you have ignored the best of yourself. While we can camouflage the outside, we can never lie to the real person on the inside. Once we can embrace the shortcomings that make us become aware that we did not allow who we truly are on the inside to fully shine at a given moment, we can continue to work on the next opportunity to showcase all that we do have to offer and then we open the door to change what is required from within. This proves the point that we can only begin with a change within ourselves.

Free To Be

Our disappointment in ourselves, and even others, can be embraced as learning curves in discovering the best of "ME."

"We are a result of the people we surround ourselves with." This statement can be used as a mirror of your best intention toward yourself and provide a reflection for you to decide if you need improvement or a total revamping.

Your inner circle can be tested by asking yourself these questions: *What did I take away from this conversation or this company? Did I make a positive or negative contribution? Does this circle contribute to my personal development and that of others?* Whatever the answer, you can decide on what you want to keep or eliminate.

Allowing the person knocking from within to emerge is challenging yourself to become what is needed or required in your circle. *What do you hold back from your circle, and if so, why are you afraid to offer it?*

The more you are able to find out what makes you tick, the more comfortable you will become around others and open and ready to thrive in your environment. Your environment consists of people who will assist you in navigating new territories for business, acquiring a new position on your job, and even making new friends and acquaintances.

We can explore the truth behind the things that hinder us as we begin to ask ourselves some questions such as:

- *Am I selfish and not wish for others to get ahead of me?*
- *Do I know how to provide honesty without argument or feelings of hurt?*
- *Can I honestly admit that I do not have it all together and I need help?*
- *Will I be ridiculed if I share my fears?*
- *Who will love me?*

As you delve into the heart of the person on the inside, "Me," you start to become refined and also gain insights on how to navigate the terrains of life by embracing the bumps in the road and celebrating the victories of one accomplishment after another.

Growth demands that you do not join the "army of blame-shifting" as it will cause you to deflect responsibility to someone else by avoiding or downplaying the lessons that need to be learned. Enrolling in this behavior is another form of running away from the work that can only be accomplished through you. Fully emerging in the transformation is being able to take a breath and look at the old you and, yes, some parts are fabulous, awesome, and great and other parts not so perfect but take a breath in all of it and simply say, "This is ME. I am not where I am supposed to be, but I am determined to do something about it."

"And be not conformed to this world: but be ye transformed by the renewing of your mind." (Romans: 12:2a - KJV).

Look at the scripture this way; what is in the world is what is happening in the world, which is already a done deal. What needs to be transformed is what needs to emerge from you, and that can only happen by what you tell yourself and feed the soul of your mind.

Remember, the world is filled with personalities, expressions, and influences from a multitude of people. To conform to it is to conform to all their desires, needs, and ideas of what is beautiful or even perfect. Use your own unique influence and make this world conform to you as you transform it.

Ask "Will you give yourself the best life?"

Seek after what you see from deep within and write it down so you might run after it.

Knock for the door to be opened to new expectations and freedom from what you are giving yourself permission to create.

Chapter 3

Forgive And Forget - How Do I Do That?

We often receive this advice or provide these words of wisdom to others. However, to forgive and forget, which is offered in the sincerest of counsel, is a challenge that most of us struggle with universally.

Testimony

I once had a conversation with the Lord which was similar to that of a debate. I was telling God I had an issue standing before a room full of people to tell them they should forget about being hurt and just keep going when I had a difficult time doing so myself. So the question always remains, "How do I do this?"

While not attempting to be difficult, there was a strong urge to really decipher how possible it is to forgive and forget. Resolving this issue has always been a challenge because we were taught to remember everything: our A-B-Cs and 1-2-3s were drummed into our minds through songs and other exercises for us to retain and recall at a moment's notice. So, how does one tell the brain to suddenly erase pain and hurt and just forget about them?

I have always cherished the brain as a recorder, where the pause, fast-forward and play buttons repeatedly create flashbacks even when you have tried to hit the delete button on the undesirable ones. So what happens when a specific memory keeps popping up, and the hurt is still there; how then do I go about forgetting?

One of the most difficult cross we will ever bear in this life is how to break the cycle of unforgiveness quickly. When you become aware that forgiveness is one of the major keys to living a truly abundant life, this knowledge will propel you to search for the answer to the question that is presented from the very pit of you, "How can I forget the pain and hurt?" If I can, then just maybe I will do it quickly and move on with life.

Forgiveness requires that you launch an investigation on how to process what you might deem acts of unforgiveness, so you can begin to conquer any form of shackles that come to hinder you.

Forgiveness means working it out; you have to be willing to do the work.

Long after a painful deed or act is finished, you are left with the emotional wound that requires you to make a decision to work pass whatever circumstance has caused you to get to an area of drought or lack of forgiveness.

The first step in moving forward is to acknowledge what has happened and accept that you cannot change the past however difficult the pain or act you endured. Moving forward will enable you to also find closure, learn the lesson in the circumstances and situations and begin to turn them into valuable benefits. Learn what you can take away from your negative experiences and have them bring positive value to yourself, and really focus on the steps to forgive and heal.

By choosing to recognize and breathe through the moments of an unpleasant experience, you can take the time to reflect on what has happened and have the courage to verbalize or express the emotions that have surfaced, such as pain, hurt and betrayal. It is important to take a handle on yourself and recognize the feelings tied to the emotional wounds such as anger, shame, and fear.

Anger will cause you to experience physical conditions, such as increased heart rate, elevated blood pressure, and exhibit behaviors, such as being quickly vexed, irritated, cross, and exasperated.

Shame carries a painful feeling of humiliation or distress caused by a behavior or action.

Fear is an unpleasant emotion caused by the belief that someone or something is dangerous, likely to cause pain, or is a threat.

Forgiving oneself can be more difficult than forgiving someone else. There are unpleasant emotions that arise while dealing with our past; the intense sensation of being made to feel like a fool, feeling as if you were bamboozled or used can produce self-blame in being blindsided by someone else's behavior towards you. This can cause a series of distrust in your decision-making and choices.

Method 1: It is important to be able to express your thoughts and feelings in order to be clear about your emotional state. Journaling or writing allows you to freely express your experiences and voice your opinions without interruption. This gives you the freedom of having no limitations or restrictions to your expressions and permits every negative emotion to flow out of you. This gives you an opportunity to also reflect on what has affected you, the effects of what has been taking place on the inside and making a conscious decision to choose to let go and break free from the burden of holding on to pain. This can also produce not only an emotional outlet but insight into patterns of things you have been allowing in your life when you have not been paying close attention, as well as making compromising decisions that are not in standard with your self-worth.

Method 2: Another key point in the process of healing in order to forgive is to pray. Here you can express your thoughts, pain, and anger without any judgment. Praying can also provide an outlet to cry and verbalize your disappointment, disbelief, and confusion. There is nothing prayer cannot vanquish, and the release it provides from every pent-up emotion is priceless and immeasurable. Prayer offers you an opportunity to present your case to the highest court, which is in the kingdom of God. Imagine taking the witness stand, and you have the honor of giving everything over to the Lord by presenting your account. Your invitation to pray brings about a powerful connection in your relationship to become so open to share your heart. There is no judgment or cross-examination on whether you are right or wrong; you will receive the benefit of expelling everything out to your most ardent Confidante, who will handle your delicate heart with great care and love.

Presenting your frustrations and burdens in prayer also enables you to accept the next phase of your growth in letting go of any oppressive behavior and thought that would keep you stuck and bring about buckets of emptiness. Trading in bitterness for joy will enable you to accept the medicinal doses of recovery that are beneficial to you choosing the pathway of healing and becoming unstuck from the crossroad of an unwillingness to forgive.

When we allow the just Judge a moment in our affairs, we provide Him the opportunity to grace us with the path.

We cannot apply our own rules if we want to win the battle.

"Jesus answered, I tell you, not seven times, but seventy-seven times seven." (Matthew 18:22 - KJV).

Reading this scripture always brings me to a loving and humorous evaluation of my mediocre attempts at forgiveness, whether I have to apply it to myself or others. This scripture never fails to leave my eyes and mouth wide open. Having to apply biblical principles to our lives at times seems so difficult. We would want to ask God how; "Is it fair for unspeakable things to be done to me and then I have to be the better person?" Christ knew this would be one of our greatest challenges to overcome; however, He understood why it is necessary for us to put this into practice for our own good. The more readily you understand the strength in the power of letting go, the process of forgiveness will strengthen you for endless possibilities of unmerited favor and blessing; you will be able to embrace liberation and freedom. Once you allow yourself the freedom to be loosed from bondage, you too can be forgiven as you also will stumble in this journey of life.

Learn to accept that there are moments that you will not be perfect or right in all given situations, no matter how hard you try. So grasp the reality that you will not always be right. We can also begin to activate forgiveness toward the ones who crushed us.

While knowing that it is good to forgive and it releases us to live a good life, the struggle for most of us is, "How do I just forget about it?"

WE CANNOT!
WE DO NOT!
FORGET ABOUT FORGETTING!

Our memory will simply not allow us to forget because, as previously stated, it is a part of us, just like our ABCs and 123s. Since we do not forget, negative memories will always come knocking to keep us bound and stagnant, in paralysis, to prevent us from moving forward.
How do we win when this happens?

Method 3: Change the Channel - Do not dwell on it!

When flipping through the channels of your memory, if a particular occasion or memory pops up, pick up the remote and hit "NEXT."

When it flashes on your radar out of nowhere like an infomercial, just open your mouth and say, "NOT TODAY!"

There is a moment to really look over the event and analyze it from top to bottom and state, "Hey, they did me wrong, but I didn't die."

Change your position when that memory comes to take a hold of you. If you are lying down, sit up! Say out loud, "I'm sitting up now," and do it. If you are sitting, stand up and say out loud, "I'm standing up." Just simply go about changing your physical position and switch focus along with the move. As crazy as it sounds, there is always a dominant thought running around, and the uninvited ones can wreak havoc on your emotions. Therefore, if you take the opportunity to prevent another thought from coming in, you can liberate yourself to more constructive thoughts and prevent your mind, body, and spirit from being boggled down with despair.

Shame tends to carry feelings of humiliation that can lead you down a road of hopelessness. Blaming yourself for what you could have done differently to avoid some situations or encounters become pointless when you are faced with the obvious that the past cannot be changed. With these ponderings, feelings of helplessness can lead to anger and a desire to seek revenge or casting vengeance on unsuspecting persons. These persons can be blamed for not being your rescuers, and feelings of resentment and anger can project itself during the most unsuspecting occasions. This continues to create a cycle if you are unable to acknowledge what is taking place.

The event is in the past; therefore, the battle is trying to control your thoughts and becoming determined to keep this moment as a past occurrence and not one that is reoccurring and rehashing to keep you trapped. It should help you to press through and overcome so you can have a testimony that will benefit yourself and others as surviving despite the trials.

Change the channel to the here and now. Press ahead into the current movement of the present, so your focus and vision are of the good things to come and not dwelling on a past that wants to intrude and disrupt your future.

NEXT!

"Finally my brethren, whatsoever things are true, whatsoever things are honest, whatsoever things are just, whatsoever things are pure, whatsoever things are of a good report; if there be any virtue, and if there be any praise, think on these things." (Philippians 4:8 - KJV).

This scripture is a reminder that our lives are normally burdened down with thoughts that are not productive or freeing. Your thought process must become engaged in such a way that enables you to push yourself into action on a different level, wipe the drawing board clean and start again. You have full control over the shape of your minutes, hours, and day and you should work with the best efforts to accomplish that which you have set out to do. So, whenever the cobweb of imprisonment by whatever means has come set to destroy you, be reminded of the honest, just, pure and good report and pull on those memories that you may be accomplished and prosper.

Method 4: Take Control - Life has a way of throwing punches; no matter how much you have prepared and strategized, it still makes numerous attempts to take you out of the game permanently. When anything happens that will throw you off your game or distort your focus from having a fulfilled life, you must have the presence of mind to recognize when an obstacle has been thrown in your path that has come to hinder your process of fulfillment and success.

Therefore, you must begin to recognize anything or anyone taking up space in your mind that is not there to make you progress. Take a moment and check what is holding you at a stagnant place and is attempting to take root and create a stronghold in your life. The most amazing thing to discover is that fear will do its best to keep you locked in a rotational cycle of repeated unforgiveness and keep you so wrapped up in strife inside your mind. Days and weeks will pass by so quickly without you fully taking notice that you are trapped in a cycle of despair. This vicious cycle of unforgiveness will entrap you in creating an imagined world of enemies, obstacles, and lack.

Fear wrapped up in unforgiveness will hinder your progress in life. It causes mistrust of others and impedes your growth by minimizing your ability to take risks, which hinders your chance of excelling at a greater pace. Fear will not allow room for you to be shaped by experiences in a positive way when everyone around you is a suspect. This stronghold can take root (comes to oppress and bears a burden that makes focus difficult) where you will only trust persons to a point; you will only attempt new things to a point; you will have to see the outcome of everything working out precisely how you perceive it or nothing else will satisfy. Even those who are present to assist you on your journey can be hindered based on how they are perceived by you in their presentation. The attack on the mind that encompasses your thoughts and emotions will keep you trapped, thinking that everything and everyone is the enemy that has come to destroy. It also makes it seem as though staying trapped in mistrust, doubt, and anger is the place to exist; therefore, rooting you in a place of stagnancy that ends with you going nowhere but in a circle of despair.

Getting stuck in unforgiveness will delay your life from moving in a positive direction. Analyze when you have lost joy, laughter, happiness, or the zeal to be proactive and motivated in different areas of your life and you will be able to identify strongholds that want to drive you to tears, bitterness, hate, depression, and bring tiredness in the form of sleeping. Recognize that anyone of these factors will cause missed opportunities in your life because you have become unavailable to be present and participate in life today.

Anger will have you alienated from the best things.

Shame will have you question your self-worth.

Overcoming Barriers

In this game of life, we are writing our story along the way. How you handle the obstacle course is what will be remembered, stated, and written about you. You can be applauded as the one who made it pass the barrier and be saluted as the one who did not let the circumstance, person or thing keep you stuck in a pit of unforgiveness, but you kept on pressing, pushing, and working out your life. You can be remembered as the one who got back up and kept on pressing. To become such a person, you must have the determination to have a firm perspective, looking at each experience as the obstacle course through which you win over any emotion that will want to drown out your drive to live out your destiny.

Your testimony normally comes after the test; therefore, being able to recognize what has come to push you into victory requires you to suit up for a fight to win. Being devastated, blindsided, and rejected is how the test begins; however, take a minute to assess and figure out how to move beyond this, and you would have gained the right to have a testimony.

It is said that "Home is where the heart is" and the home is created by the heart of the person in whom everything resides. Your atmosphere fosters what is inside you, and it shows up in how your guests feel about their stay. Have you ever been in a home and was desperate to leave? What is fostered by the host is what greets you in their space. If the house is open and welcoming, then you feel welcomed, and you become more at ease in their home. There are times when you cannot quite place your finger on your discomfort; however, you are aware this is not a space you want to be in much longer.

Where your treasure is, there will be your heart also (See Matthew 6:21). Do not let bitterness become the portion you hold.

In quite the same way you recognize that your heart no longer aches, neither does your jaw clench over things you overcome; you will be able to recognize and embrace your supporters, who can applaud your victory when you have truly weathered and battled a storm. They will be able to rejoice as witnesses to the building of your strength.

Creating new habits for your mental and emotional well-being is critical to engage your mind in constructive ways that will empower you to view yourself in a positive light. Remind yourself of the good qualities you possess and continue to work on broadening your horizon with all you have to learn. At first, it might seem difficult to take on; however, building on the framework to propel you to a better place will be truly beneficial eventually.

There is nothing like the present to engage in a new hobby. Place your focus on learning to play chess, learning how to sew, creating a beautiful flower garden, turn your hand at growing your own vegetables; anything can bring a new focus and balance to replace something that yields no productive fruit to something that can bring you pleasure and satisfaction.

Explore Self Love

You can secretly be hiding from yourself, not even recognizing when you have fallen out of love with yourself. Can you imagine walking around and being afraid to really embrace yourself in the mirror? Yes, you groom yourself; however, you are not quite looking yourself in the eye. All this is clearly telling you that there is something you need to find from within yourself, to gently and lovingly say, *"Hey you, I love you, and I have been here with you all along. Somethings we did well, and somethings, oh my! Some great and wonderful things we have experienced and some things we barely survived or if we survived. Guess what? I still love you!"*

One side of the coin of self-love and forgiveness is feeling foolish for allowing a deed or act to be inflicted on you or even letting yourself down for whatever reason. Accepting that you are living and growing through life and all your experiences, desirable or not, will begin to shape who you choose to become despite the circumstances.

Stand in front of the mirror and look at yourself. Call yourself by your full name and whatever is in your heart, speak it to yourself. Whatever you need to get rid of, calling yourself by name, declare that this is the day you rid yourself of that thing. If you are being truthful about making a change, you will feel a sense of relief to know you are facing one of your pains and you are releasing its hold on you. Begin to replace the undesirables with beautiful affirmations. *"Beautiful one, I see you, and I see the stars aligning in your favor. Your future has never looked so bright, and I am rooting for you."*

Self-love will allow you to forgive your shortcomings and still be encouraged to move on. Guess what? You will find others who will also help you do this along the way.

How To Be Free And Testify

One of the first lessons that a new driver is taught by the instructor when getting around the wheel of a car is to focus on where you are going, and automatically you will steer the car in the direction it needs to go. Always remember, wherever the eye goes, the car goes.

The body will follow where the mind goes; therefore, what you focus on becomes a part of the very essence of what shows up on the outside, and it expresses itself in your facial expressions and even your body language.

Taking control of your thoughts is sitting in the driver's seat of your life and steering with complete focus on the direction you need to go. Begin to focus on what you are responsible for and do not become entrapped in your past. Focusing on the present forces you to participate in life and, therefore, creates a distance between stagnant memories and a productive life.

You have a license to be free and conquer!

Ask "Will I be free to unburden myself from the shackles?"

Seek ways that will allow you to win over your obstacles.

Knock so that you can step through the door of being an overcomer.

Chapter 4

Words Have Power ~ You Have Power With Your Words

Words are very important, and they have power. However, we sometimes find it intimidating to put them into action in our own lives. There are moments when failing to find the right words will leave conversations strained and tensions rising because of the unspoken word. We tend to have words trapped in the thought process that can run awry in our minds if we do not permit ourselves the freedom to speak. Most times, we can have internalized dialogue that never generates into a full conversation because we are fearful of the outcome. You are mindful not to wander in a direction that was not expressed and avoid confusion between yourself and others.

However, you need to communicate in order to share with others your opinions, needs and desires which enable you to see and hear yourself. Your willingness to engage in conversation will enable you to recognize the state you are in currently.

Silence is needed to bring balance and serenity to your very spirit and soul. You can utilize silence for reflection and measure your actions and words, which will show you how great a day you have experienced or what can be done for improvement. Take a moment to go over your day and what interactions became available, and how you handled yourself in the process. This provides a space to investigate the areas of self-improvement that need to be part of your daily walk as you prepare to go into the next day and the future encounters that you can navigate more effectively.

There is a difference between having a quiet nature and remaining quiet because of nerves. You can remain quiet out of insecurity, where you believe your knowledge is limited, and you cannot provide any substance to a conversation. There are moments you have already experienced when you did not speak, you were not heard and others definitely did not hear you. Allowing your voice to be heard will enable others to understand you better. When you are able to engage in conversations, then you are also able to declare your positions and boundaries.

The Flip Side Of Speaking

"Sticks and stones may break my bones, but words can never harm me" is absolutely false. Words have the power to build you up or break you down. Words can cause a smile to come across your face, and they can also bring you to tears which can stem from joy, anger, or pain from words spoken.

As we begin to speak, there can be a clear reflection of where we are in our current thought process.

Analyze your thoughts and ensure they are healthy.

The impact of words can shape who you become and what you believe about yourself. We can become scarred by the words that are spoken over us or to us.

Death and life are in the power of the tongue, and those who love and indulge it, will eat its fruit and bear the consequences of their words. (See Proverbs 18:21).

Whatever you need established begins with the words that you speak, so move above silence and speak. Begin to understand the power of your words.

And Jacob vowed a vow, saying, if God will be with me, and will keep me in this way that I go, and will give me bread to eat and raiment to put on, so that I come again to my father's house in peace; then shall the Lord be my God. (Genesis 28:20-21 – KJV)

Jacob had lived a very secure life; however, the decisions that he made caused him to have to depart from his father's house. This process started him on a journey of maturity, which also led him to establish his relationship with God. He also began to come into covenant with God.

To understand this scripture is to grasp the importance of the opportunity given to you, that you can use your words to create and establish your life with purpose.

The open secret is in the revelation that you create your own life with the words you speak. You must consider the words that you will speak since they shape your existence. One of the things to understand in shaping your words is to become honest and truthful when it comes to words you use about yourself. Your words or self-talk come from your thoughts and the words formed in your mind about yourself. These words either inspire or deflate your spirit, creating a positive or negative image of you, and this reflects what you truly believe about yourself. The words you speak to others either build them up or cuts them down. It is your responsibility to choose what you do with your words as it pertains to others.

Your words can often be used as weapons without you being fully aware of the damage being done. Then there are scenarios where you are fully aware of the effects of your words. Words once spoken can never be taken back; therefore, you are forever marked by what you have out there.

Become purposeful with your words about yourself, and you will see just how you can bring your life into focus to accomplish your dreams and desires. You will begin to recognize how magnetic your words are and the type of people who become drawn to you to present experiences and opportunities to your life. When you take a moment to be still, you will recognize how they were drawn to you, whether out of fear or hope. Knowing that you have powerful thoughts and words running around in your brain will reflect what is attracted to you. This should make you question just what you have been entertaining in your thoughts and creating with your words that have brought this particular thing into your life.

Ponder on this thought for a moment: a pleasant person surrounds himself with pleasant thoughts and pleasant circumstances. A pleasant person's mindset is set on endless positive outlooks and experiences that will generate pleasant and joyous memories in the future. This individual is also different from a worrisome person who has the mindset that something is going to go wrong, which brings even more worry.

A conversation with both or either individuals concerning the possible outcome of an event can inspire a positive and focused individual to attend. This individual may believe that he or she will surely meet wonderful people and have a great experience at the event. On the flip side of the coin, the conversation could go differently where the other individual is fearful that something terrible will happen. Either way, the experience will be truthful in how the event turns out based on one's perspective. One would simply enjoy the event, having looked forward to a positive experience because the individual's mindset was in that direction, and the other person would have been worried the entire time, looking for something to go wrong. Being consumed by worry can cause us to miss life's moments.

Setting a standard must bring about a conviction, which is a belief that every cell you possess accepts this new standard to be true.

Your thoughts and words must come in alignment in order to secure your convictions to becoming a replication of your best self for usefulness to yourself and others. You must be truthful of the words and the self-talk that has brought you to this place. However, it is now time to recognize the ones that no longer serve a purpose in your life if you intend to grow up to another level. You must have the conviction that whatever magnet your thoughts, words, and actions have provided up to this current point, they must honor where you are going in the future. Your thoughts must change so your speech can change, and your actions will be guided in the direction of where your next experience should take you to serve a greater purpose. Examine your convictions and determine if whether these convictions are about yourself and others. Measure if you want to stick with these convictions or if they need to be changed.

When you have become frustrated in the position you are in, you must check your thoughts and self-talks. Take the time to find a quiet corner or space and give yourself a self-talk check-up. Evaluate if you have been frustrated or satisfied with the direction your life has been taking. Whatever the result, check the words of inspiration or oppression that have been walking around and serving your mind in fruitfulness or fruitlessness.

Have a foundation of where you are coming from:

- I am blessed to be a blessing: I am a blessing.
- I am amazing: I learn new things.
- I am going to be a great friend: I am a great friend.
- I am going to change my career.
- I am going to stick to an exercise routine: I am sticking to an exercise routine.
- I am going to be a great mom: I am a great mom.
- I am going to explore the world.

Getting stuck in a rut where conversation is taken hostage in your thoughts is a very easy place to regress. However, always become cognizant of where you are going so you do not feel as if you are trying to catch up.

Remember, silence is your choice, and it is a privilege to know when it is vital to be still. However, never be silenced into dumbness and never be silenced to count yourself out of the game. You must be inclined to figure out where you are, where you are going, what is required to stay there, and what is required to push ahead. Your progress comes from opening your mouth and asking appropriate questions.

Be bold enough to ask for assistance along the way and be courageous enough to just engage in a conversation about the butterfly, sky, or simply someone's dress or tie. Giving a compliment is one of the biggest ice breakers. Someone is always in need of a smile formed from the words of friendship, kindness, and joy. Let whatever you have to give in the smallest of measures be said in the greatest of treasures from your heart. You must know that when you are placed somewhere, your statements are going to speak for themselves, so let them speak good and honest things.

Whatever comes from your heart to your lips should reflect who you choose to be so you do not live in regret or constantly having to sieve over your words. You are here to offer love, kindness, advice, and encouragement. Let the pureness of who you are speak, and you will not regret your words.

There are places in time when your words will begin to return to you in measures you cannot possibly imagine, and they will come back to you with the truthfulness in which you sent them out. Words are indeed magnetic and powerful; therefore, speak, even when you have a nervous stomach.

We have butterflies in our stomach not because we have nothing to say; sometimes we stay quiet out of fear because we think what we have to say is irrelevant or we do not have any right to an opinion. However, our positions and even our relationships are either limited or enhanced by the words we speak. So where are we?

Understanding that the quality of our words defines us can empower us to become more responsible with our conversations and speech. Connecting your words to engage on the very basic levels, even with a child, can become so freeing and enlightening that as you can speak, you can begin to live through your words.

When you allow yourself to speak, it brings a sound and a presence to your surroundings that represent your unique identity. Lending your voice to an opinion, advice, and encouragement speaks volumes to your self-confidence and assurance that your voice and words add value. You have been given a voice to communicate and not to be silenced because of fear.

Speaking allows you the opportunity to evaluate your interactions and encounters. This gives you permission to declare, "I shall speak and no longer be silent so that I can hear myself." If I am happy, I will hear it by the words I speak. If I am sad, it will show through how I carry my words. Therefore, whatever is happening will show up so you can be encouraged or push yourself to improve your communication skills. In doing this, you add more value to yourself and social structures, which consists of your friends, family, and working environment.

Tip: Reading a book of interest can become a great avenue and a conversation piece with a total stranger, who will generate a conversation just based on the topic of a book. This simple move can become a great tool to provide you with opportunities of growing your circle of friends and acquaintances by the books you read.

A conversation piece can come from the lettering on a t-shirt, whether it is something of interest to discuss commonality or the conversation can be based on the curiosity of a logo. It can stem from a compliment given by someone or extending the same to someone else. The liberty to speak and declare that you are lacking in experience or knowledge can be used as a tool for new adventures, opening the door to the teacher or teachers who will enter your life and guide you to the next level of teaching.

Children are some of our greatest teachers if we allow them. They can provide you with insight on how you communicate and often provide you with areas that need improvement. To be told that you are not listening with your eyes by a child simply lets you know that your undivided attention is required. This leads to one of the most important points to consider as well as a vital question to ask oneself, "Am I a good listener?"

Becoming a good listener will allow you to know what is needed in conversations and enables you to be proactive. You can discern if someone just needs an ear to vent and make yourself available just to listen, and you can determine if someone is genuinely seeking advice. The ability to be a good listener will definitely assist you in using the right note to strike up a conversation. All of this can bring you to a place of comprehension, to provide you with insight on whether what you communicated was understood.

People who speak will build their confidence:

- Know your limitations by knowing yourself and how a disability can limit your functionality. You can help others better understand you and how you best function. Be secure enough to engage others.

People who speak up inspire others:

- Know your rights and responsibilities. Use and find resources; know what you need so you can recognize who and where to get it from.

Believe in yourself enough to define your words, so they are reflected to you in powerful measures that bring transformation, care, love, loyalty, beauty, passion, selflessness, worthiness, determination, engagement, humor, laughter, joy.

Evaluation: For most of my working life, I have been giving end-of-year self-evaluations with guidelines to grade myself "fairly" and never give myself too high a score because it will show favorable bias; therefore, not providing room for critique. I started thinking about these rules and guidelines that were to be followed while keeping in mind that others were being given the opportunity to give their own assessment based on their opinion of my work, and I had no control over their "fair" evaluation. Fair evaluations took on a new meaning when I made the decision to fully evaluate and rank myself at the highest level and stated why my high opinion of myself was worth the consideration. I began to make a conscious effort to live up to my evaluation that they might remain truthful to the value I had placed on my ranking. I purposed myself to write objectives that challenged me quarterly and then noted what I could do better, which was to improve on new discoveries of my work and potential.

Be very clear about what you need to say and have that conversation even when you are fearful. Having a conversation means you have the mindfulness to show up and make your declarations known. It creates a statement that you are able to set a task and complete your goals no matter what they might be.

They will show up again to you. You will get to see the effects and the lives changed as you begin to master what you do with them. You will begin to hear the testimonies when you have spoken with care and when you have been careless. Either way, they will show up again and again.

So shall my word be that goeth forth out of my mouth; it shall not return unto me void, but it shall accomplish that which I please, and it shall prosper in the thing whereto I sent it. (Isaiah 55:11 - KJV).

This is such a profound reminder that we are formed in the likeness and image of God and, by His very breath, He gave us life. Therefore, the very words that we speak, God has given us the power to breathe life into them. How we speak and what we say becomes attached to us, and it is being magnified as an extension of us. Do we create life or death with our words, or do we construct death and destruction? Whether we are speaking to ourselves or to others, the very breath of our words have power.

By extension, your words will accomplish all that you have sent them to do. Therefore, become charged, so the words you speak are a light of hope and joy to the world. Let your words be seasoned with flavor that they return to you in good and bountiful measures.

We are changed by the words of our mouth!

Ask "When I begin to know myself, will I know what to ask for?"

Seek: As you begin to progress, you will know what you are seeking after. One set course might not take you to your destiny; however, if you keep seeking and moving, it will certainly provide you with the proven life experience.

Knock on the door of expectation because that is a sure possibility for it to open to you.

Chapter 5

Laugh At Yourself A Lot ~ Going Through The Waves

Being able to laugh at your own self is freedom. Being able to have others laugh at your situation or experience is liberating. Liberation and freedom come with the discovery and acceptance that you are going to experience some unavoidable mishaps. Do you realize that the pressure to please others can keep you focused on getting outside approvals? This can make us live a strained, rigid, black and white life of right and wrong, which in essence makes us BORING!

Explore this notion and see where it takes you.

Discovery

If you have ever been to the beach, whether just to lie on the sand to soak in some sun or take a swim, you will notice the ripples or rolls on the water defined as waves. A wave, as defined in physics, is a regular recurring event, such as a surf coming in

Free To Be

toward a beachfront, and can even be thought of as a disturbance. Waves are usually characterized by wavelength, frequency, and the speed at which they move.

A wave can be considered thrilling or terrifying based on an individual's perspective. A wave rider, otherwise called a surfer, rides the face of a moving wave that carries the surfer towards the shore. If you are in the rhythm of a wave, you can move seamlessly with it and enjoy the thrill, speed, and height of the ride while anticipating how far the wave will take you. If you are not prepared for a wave, it can really take you for a rough and tumble ride. Either joyride or wipe out, whichever one happens, would you be able to cherish the experience?

My Story

Many moons ago, I went to the beach with my friend, Bern, who had just purchased the sports car of his dreams. I told him that whenever he was not busy, I wanted a ride to the beach in his beautiful car with the top down. He finally took me up on my offer one gorgeous sunny afternoon.

Mind you, I am a beach poser, not a swimmer, and it took me forever to get into the water on that beautiful day. While I was enjoying my lounge time on the shore, after a while, my friend started beckoning me to join him in the water, and I started my swimsuit model walk. As I started wading in, a huge wave came crashing over me; I swallowed water, and the wave picked me up and kept tossing me back towards the shore. Needless to say, I came up looking like a wet cat being dunked unwillingly. After several attempts, I gained my footing and gathered enough dignity to rise up again and continue to walk towards Bern as if this was all part of the plan. I saw my friend diligently searching for me and, by the expression on his face, probably decided he needed to call a lifeguard. When he finally spotted me, and I assured him that I was fine, he laughed so hard because I am sure I looked like a cartoon character. One moment I was standing, and then, in the blink of an eye, I had disappeared under the massive blanket of water and resurfaced looking like the aftermath of a tornado.

I called my friend a few years later to have a joint laughter in what I considered to be one of my most embarrassing moments, and, to my surprise, he did not remember what happened. He chuckled as I described the moment again and again. This confirmed that while it was funny, there was no recollection of my fall of shame in his memories.

I had a light bulb moment as I recognized that while we are focused on what others think, they have their own moments they are concerned about. Therefore, what was of great concern and embarrassment to me was a non-existent memory in my friend's mind.

How did I treat this memory? As a badge of honor, declaring I can fall down and be embarrassed at times, but I am also able to get back up and even laugh at myself.

I heard this quote by Jim Rohn: "You must let life hit you, but you must not let it kill you." The message was so profound that it immediately brought a reminder of the scripture:

"For everything there is a season, and a time for every purpose under heaven. A time to be born, and a time to die; a time to plant, and a time to pluck up that which is planted, a time to kill, and a time to heal, a time to break down and a time to build up, a time to weep and a time to laugh, a time to mourn, and a time to dance." (Ecclesiastes 3:1-4 - KJV).

This scripture is such a sound reminder that no matter how great you navigate and plan your life, no one can endure forever in one season, and every part of life will touch you as an individual. Moments in life will present different types of waves that show up as the highs and the lows in our journey, and they will all require you to deal with them in different ways. Having and keeping a healthy perspective on life will keep us alert. Being alert will also allow you to become mindful of the best tools needed to go through the waves. Life must be lived to its fullest in ways that make your life filled with meaning.

Every wave comes with its own set of challenges, and each one has its solution attached to it, no matter how hopeless some might appear at times. There must be a commitment to being involved in the entire process so that you will be able to see your way through. You are required to figure out what is the best way for you to deal with the storms that appear because you will still crash and burn or ride a wave.

Waves can be as simple as moving to a new location, which will cause you to develop new patterns of getting to work, finding the supermarket, meeting new neighbors, and whatever else it takes for you to feel at home in your new neighborhood. It might take no time or a little while to find your footing, but eventually, with routine and a new pattern, you will cruise on this wave of life with your eyes closed.

Another wave can come in the form of losing a loved one, which no matter how prepared we are, the loss can leave us devastated and experiencing such grief that it makes you feel as if parts of you are missing. Finding the right coping methods in order to help you handle loss effectively can make you available to be empathetic and even helpful to others in their moments of loss.

Passing and coming through events has laughing moments, whether negative or positive.

Develop the skill to deal with waves. Do not get caught up in moments of inferiority, but press towards the best way to come out with more clarity and understanding of all your dark places.

The power of laughter has some really good benefits. It decreases stress hormones and increases immune cells and infection-fighting anti-bodies; therefore, improving your resistance to disease. Your laughter triggers the release of endorphins, the body's natural feel-good chemicals which stimulate many organs. Laughter enhances your intake of oxygen-rich air, stimulates your heart, lungs, and muscles, and increases the endorphins that are released by your brain. The benefits of laughter include:

- Soothes tension.
- Improves your immune system.
- Relieves pain.
- Helps you connect with people and deal with difficult situations.
- Stimulates organs and increases endorphins.
- Improves your mood.
- Burns calories.
- Increases blood flow.

With all these great benefits, what is there not to laugh about? It is good to be reminded of what can be gained by laughing, even at yourself. One of the best medicines is laughter, and it is so good for your soul to be nourished by it. Having a good chuckle and knowing that someone else can benefit from your laughter is also a great privilege to offer such a gift.

There is therefore now no condemnation to them which are in Christ Jesus, who walk not after the flesh, but after the Spirit. (Romans 8:1 - KJV).

This scripture is simply a reminder that brings comfort that there is nothing that brings humiliation to you that you cannot escape or get over when you allow yourself the liberty which Christ has given. Anything created or spoken should not be able to trap you in such a burdensome place that you cannot escape.

Challenge yourself to look back on some moments that you might not have found funny at the time and open yourself to even reminisce by yourself or share with someone and just laugh out loud about the matter. Give yourself the honor of saying, "Yeah, that was not so good," and be able to keep it moving.

Making a retreat into dormancy because of a mistake is standing on the shore and never testing the water of trials to see how you will get to the other side.

Can you imagine Jesus having a sense of humor? Entering Christendom can sometimes feel restrictive. Jesus, in His narrative, kindly reminds us that it is not the outward showing that we should concern ourselves with, but rather the things in our heart that show up in our actions and deeds. He did not concern Himself much with trivial matters. He tended to address the matter at hand and then move on.

It brings us back to the analysis that when waves hit, you can be swept off your feet and unexpectedly find yourself taking in water and being thrown completely off balance until the speed of the wave has completed its task and crashed fully to shore, sometimes taking you with it.

In life, we are always in the midst of a wave, which sometimes comes in the form of a ripple that is hardly noticeable and has no real impact on your life. The waves that can bring us crashing to shore unexpectedly while trying not to take in a big gulp of the sea are the ones we can either face head-on or we drown under the pressure.

Creating memories and moving through experiences requires us to ride some waves. Waves, whether we call them interruptions or delights, if taken in proper perspectives of growth in our lives, will propel us to having a memory-filled journey. Dust off some of those wishful thoughts and just put your foot in the water.

Whichever end of the spectrum we end up, it is okay to laugh in triumph or smile at the silliness of it all. Either way, the wave also comes at us as a part of our life; some we ride successfully, and others come to give us a crash landing to shore or a wake-up call. Guess what? The wave dissipates, and it disappears, and we are left with an experience and a memory.

You have to remember to laugh through it!

Here comes another wave!

Ask "Have I seen this wave before? How will I ride it?"

Seek: Where will this wave take me, and what will assist me in riding on top and not beneath it?

Knock out the waves as quickly as they come so you can begin to ride with the experience.

Chapter 6

Dream A Little – It Will Take You Somewhere

A dream is considered to be a series of thoughts, images, and sensations occurring in a person's mind during sleep. Another aspect of a dream is to contemplate the possibility of actively bringing a dream or a vision to life.

While the former deals with the subconscious, at the moment, it is more beneficial to observe the latter, which we consider as being more under our control and, therefore, we are able to contemplate endless possibilities for ourselves. Dreams place an expectation on us to cultivate something new in our surroundings, and they prompt us to explore how to become innovative and adventurous. The most wonderful thing about your dream is that you are the creator and designer of what will be transformed from thought to reality.

Will you decide to make your dream become a part of your reality?

As an adult, you may realize that the dreams or fantasies you had as a child were your life aspirations waiting on you to come true. Often, as you begin to proceed through life, your dreams can begin to seem so unattainable and, if you are not watching, you will not realize that it was all possible and is still possible. You are just in need of the proper roadmap to achieving your dream(s).

Testimony

"Along life's way, a part of me stopped living and just started being part of a machine." I became a cog in the wheel that just did routine without the joy. Was I miserable? Not really; however, I was not happy and or fulfilled because the light and the child in me, who would dream and envision life in the fullest, got misplaced while trying to fit into everything and become whatever that was to everyone else.

One morning, while living in my apartment, as beautiful as it was, I started desiring grass, and as I looked to capture where I wanted to live, I knew I wanted to feel grass beneath my feet. I wanted to view the terrain and the territory and just take a nice breath of fresh air and look out at nature. I started looking at homes around the local areas and nothing was satisfying the fire that had been lit on the inside of me. Parts of me were satisfied, but nothing that would propel change. Things changed when we pulled up to this yard that had the loveliest surroundings of what I desired.

However, sitting in the center of the most beautiful landscape was one of the ugliest looking houses I had ever seen.

I told my brother I would truly sit this one out since it was a cold day and felt like a complete waste of time. I was finally convinced to go take a look inside, and the moment I did, I fell head over heels in love with this shell of a home, which now had the greatest potential and the most spectacular ocean view. I did not want to leave. I took this shell of a house and literally created, with my brilliant mind, the spectacular masterpiece that could be done only by the master renovators that would come in the form of experienced architects and contractors.

Disappointment set in when I was outbid by a contractor and it became difficult to fill my eyes and heart again for a while. Bigger or smaller, nothing grabbed a hold of me, and through all of the ups and downs of finding a home, I chose to move into the basement of my brother's home because there was a determination not to renew my apartment lease. Signing up to renew my stay there would be putting my dreams and desires on hold for something that was just not satisfying to me any longer. It was a nerve-wracking experience sharing space with someone again, much less sharing space with children!

It took a year before settling into my dream home. During that year, my spiritual and emotional life went through a transition and transformation. That year brought me into an analyzing perspective of myself, and I am always amazed that all I wanted to do was move out of my apartment into a home and touching grass outside. Along this path, life threw along some curveballs that matured and gave me insights into myself that would have been left untapped. The inquisitiveness of children turned me into a more understanding human being; however, there was also the discovery that things that easily brought frustration became a mere lint, if noticeable at all.

While going through the process of looking for my dream home, our church went through a church split that devastated me to my core. I was hurt to a proportion that I thought I would never recover. The pain went deep, and I felt like someone had cut me with a knife. It was devastating because the split involved some of my family members, which compounded the hurt and hurled me into a place of anger and unforgiveness. Family, for me, is always a bond that no matter what we go through, there is nothing we cannot survive together. Having the people I held dear to my heart walk away felt like a betrayal of my perspective of everything I held to be true. This made me question everything about myself, who I thought I was, and my own level of understanding in anything I did.

I had to go back to the drawing board of my life and check if indeed I was still capable of being a kind, compassionate, forgiving, and loving individual and leaving myself to answer the question, if my family was important enough to me. Despite our difference of opinions, no matter how painful, I had to determine if the experience was a valid excuse to cut ties and call it quits to justify my feelings of being wronged. I had to understand that whatever emotions came with my feelings of betrayal had to be resolved by me and not by my family or anyone else. Another discovery in deciding who I was going to be was still my responsibility.

Family is a big part of what defines me, and coming to the realization that in the midst of pushing to grasp one dream, something that I had been blessed with, such as a close-knit family, was likely to be shattered by this trial. It became necessary to see and choose whether I could become a key component in family preservation or destruction.

Hindrances will appear in whatever form to keep you stuck from moving forward with your plans with any sense of joy and accomplishment. The process of reconciliation has been an uphill battle; however, it is one that I do not shy away from, ensuring that whatever the enemy wanted for bad, my God will turn it around for good. I became determined to root up, pull down, and destroy weeds that came in the form of generational curses that showed up as misunderstanding, revenge, and unforgiveness. Then I planted, built up, and restored flowers of joy and fellowship back to their beautiful status.

Through it all, I became confident in my understanding of who I was shaping up to *become*, taking responsibility for who I was (the good and not so good parts of me) and what I would not compromise. Even going through the process of developing, and with time and effort, there was still a push inside of me not to cancel my dream of attaining joy and happiness due to the trials that came.

Once a dream is awakened on the inside of you, it then begins to press you to do something about your situation in order for change to come. Even when you are afraid, the dream keeps creeping in on you to let you know that in order to be free from fear, you must address whatever you are afraid of. Whatever needs to be accomplished must take some effort on your part. Dreams, whether classified as a nightmare or hope, provides you the opportunity to deal with yourself and how you see yourself.

Our dreams are most alive when we are children, and the responsibilities of life can forever beat them into almost non-existence; however, it is the hope and potential of these dreams that truly keep the spirit within us alive.

Making the word of God a habitual part of your day becomes a necessary vitamin to your soul. The word brings reassurance and cancels worry in order for you to become who you were born to become by engaging you in the process of life with zeal and passion. Finding the messages that bring substance to your life enables you to push even more towards working on your goals so that your dreams can come true.

"Eye has not seen, nor ear heard, Nor have entered into the heart of man the things which God has prepared for those who love him." (1 Corinthians 2:9 - KJV).

The beauty of this scripture is the encouragement to always have the inquisitive and earnest expectation of a child and never allow your imagination to grow dim that your belief in great expectations diminishes. Your belief and expectation are the ultimate key to heaven because the Lord will move heaven and earth for you to receive what you desire. When you allow that youthful imagination to always be a part of you, all things, even through the ups and downs, will be working toward your good.

At some point when you begin to take notice, you realize that your dream enlightens you to everything that connects to the subconscious thoughts inside of you. Whether you feel like you are being chased or see yourself flying, it signifies something that is happening or taking place in your world, and it is calling your attention to the matter at hand. At times, it will become so forceful that you are pushed to take responsibility to find out what it all means for you.

Your dreams and aspirations come to bring awareness that your walk, even though the path may be crowded, is yours alone to take. The people and the decisions along the way are what make up your life story. They are counted as steps which we call memories and connections, and eventually they lead you to fulfill your purpose so your dreams might come to pass.

Life is best lived when there is expectation bursting forth from inside of you. An idea to design and sew an outfit, designing a room, writing a song, or simply driving to another city can fill your imagination with countless ways of how these can be accomplished. Living for a future and a hope is what drives one to wake up in the morning and look forward to a fulfilling day. Keeping the imagination sharp and filled with excitement as a child waiting for Christmas morning will push you to meet and surpass any challenge that comes up. Your future must always have something on the horizon to look forward to and attain. It should fill you with hope and challenge your mind on how you are going to get there.

"Fight the good fight of faith..." (1 Timothy 6:12a – KJV).

This word of encouragement reminds me that anything good does not come free, and everything good is worth seeing through to the end. Standing up for what you believe in must be strongly rooted in you, even when you are the only one who believes it. In this moment, you will be the one nurturing this seed so it does not get plucked out of the ground before having the opportunity to take root.

The doubts and questions will arise and challenge you on whether the dream is worth the struggle. One of the most important hurdles to climb over is the mental exercise of struggling to figure out how to perfect everything and never starting anything, which will cause a delay in your destiny and future.

Destinations to fulfilling your dreams are paved with obstacles called transformational stories. We must allow them to assist us by embracing our learning curves and acquiring the experiences needed for the necessary steps of our journey. No one remains the same at the beginning of learning a new skill and when they become an expert in a subject matter.

Asking is key on this journey!

We are not going to know all the answers, but being courageous by asking questions with the curiosity of a little child fully expecting to be answered, guided and assisted, will take us one step closer to where we ought to go. If there is a need to be fulfilled, then someone is out there looking to fulfill that need.

If you have a dream, a vision, and a destiny, that means you are not there yet. Therefore, think of your dreams as a place where you need to arrive. Every obstacle and failure shape you into the image and character of your destination.

Remember, challenges and obstacles follow those on the pathway to success.

Ask someone who has succeeded in their dreams to tell you their story.

Seek out how to go about making your dream a reality.

Knock on the door of your dreams and imaginations, and let them out.

Chapter 7

Own You

I laugh out loud (lol) all the time, not just as an expression via text, but I literally laugh where people can hear me. I embrace my whim to laugh and express genuine joy. I laugh at the storyline of a good book; I laugh at a good joke; I love to laugh, and I do it freely, softly, and sometimes full out without apology.

In this world of social media, we tend to share emojis (expressions) as conversations and never participate in the joys of exhibiting our true selves or feelings. Now that we tend to replace true expressions with emotional icons, our eyes can become distorted with a delusion of what is normal. With this behavior, we begin to compete with a façade created by others, that we sometimes compare our lives to what seems acceptable but have not tested the authenticity of the source to which we compare our worth in order to express our genuine thoughts and emotions. At times, we try to fit so perfectly "in" that we rule ourselves "out" and think we do not carry value.

Some individuals come along understanding their value in life or, at least, what it takes to live to their fullest potential. Others are late bloomers and can get lost or even confused defining what they are or should become.

Comparing ourselves with others has its benefits, and seeing someone's positive attributes should cause us to honor our self-worth and display our own. No one or no thought process should diminish you to mediocrity or paralysis that may cause you to live and operate on a level that will reflect a sub-standard existence. Being creatures of habit can cause us to unconsciously adapt to others' behavior and personality. The most impressive you can get lost and continue as never seeing, never establishing or never developing your true self because you have quietly transitioned into someone and something that you are not.

Owning you is to take control of yourself and take yourself back from anything that wants to keep you as a hostage. What do I mean by hostage? I am referring to whatever captivates your thought process and makes you question the very first step that has been given to you by the Holy Spirit to move, speak, say a word and break free from what has kept you stuck in the first place. As we worry and ponder where our minds might lead us and what might happen, we actually end up being imprisoned by just a thought. Wow! How powerful it will be to give yourself free will to express yourself in love, care, and honesty. We can become depressed when we lack the ability to express who we are or if we have somehow lost our identity along the way, and even worse, the sad part can be when we do not know when it happened.

Testimony

We either go or move through life not quite fitting into our "skin." We adapt and conform to ways and ideas, and sometimes we are bold enough to already come or reach that point and move at a steadfast pace with it. However, each man walks their own mile.

The Bible tells us it is better to visit the house of mourning than to go to the house of feasting, for that is the end of all men (See *Ecclesiastes 7:2 – KJV*). There are two persons in my life who influenced me in their own way. I was in the process of life lessons without even knowing it.

My grandmother, Albertha Benjamin, affectionately known as Sissy, lived till she decided it was time to leave this earth. It was an honor for me to hear her speak to God with her hands in the air and say, "Lord, take me, I am ready."

She had a working life and, from the moments I recall, not an easy one. There were times the hospital was home, and her home was a one-night visit before heading back to the hospital the next day. As a child, I would come home from school with expectations of great joy to learn that she was home or be disappointed that she could not make it home because of severe asthma.

Even when Sissy was just able to lie in bed propped up with a pillow, her presence made everyone feel happier that she was around. Luckily, that was just the younger years of my life, and my Sissy grew stronger and, I would say, fighting and beating asthma at a distance.

If I had to describe her, strength comes to mind. Even when she was ill, she was in charge. She was my hero because when there was bullying going on at school, I knew I had a champion at home who would stand in my corner. Survival of the fittest does not warrant your parents telling you to inform a teacher and let them handle a situation. Survival of the fittest makes you boldly declare that you have a grandmother who will come fight for you, who will meet you half way from your school route, or who will stand at the gate and declare "no one touches you and live." She was truly my champion, plus she taught me a few survival skills that will remain a secret so my mother will be able to maintain her sanity, even now.

Outside of being my champion, there was no one in need that she did not help, even if it meant sharing her asthma inhaler; her plate made room for anyone who was hungry and stopped by unexpectedly (this trait is still not manifested in me).

She flourished as a businesswoman who ran her own storefront for years until the day she decided it was time to travel abroad and allow her children and grandchildren to cater to her. It was during these times with her that I began to value her life experiences. She believed and trusted God and had a faithful and consistent prayer life and firmly believed that if she asked for something and spoke it with conviction, then the Lord would make it happen for her. When she spoke, she purposed in her heart and allowed it to come to pass. One of my constant reminders of her conversation is that she spoke to God and said, "Let me get a man who will be my husband and who will be the father of all my children, and I will serve in one church," and so it happened.

She gave me practical life lessons that made me avoid looking at life with rose-colored glasses, but to dose on it with love, goodness and kindness. She impacted my life enough that my love, respect, and appreciation for her made me come home to her when it was her time to transition.

Adelaide Henry was my great-grandmother. She was of Syrian descent, and I would go visit her often in the summertime because she had sweet ripe bananas to spare, and then I would step into her closet and play dress up.

She believed in God and the Word of God, and if you should scan through her Bible with all its highlights, you can see the trust and peace that she had in serving her God. A magnifying glass replaced her glasses later on so she could go over scriptures that were near and dear to her. Even though all her children resided in foreign countries, she chose never to travel outside of her country, Jamaica. When asked if she had any desire to just get away, she would always say, "If God wanted me to fly, he would have given me wings." How could you possibly win against such an argument? She was the fanciest looking housewife on her way to church on Sunday mornings. Being a fancy church goer, there were long wigs and short wigs, pearls, high heels, and kitten heels, and I had a field day in her closet, looking at myself in the mirror and also trying to walk with a steady gait down the hallway in those heels.

While I loved her, I never appreciated her until I understood the value of life. She made me laugh loads just by her facial expressions and her tone in delivering a joke. A smile was always on her face, and she was fully satisfied and content with her simple way of life. She lacked nothing since her happiness and joy came from within. The only time I had ever seen her sad was from the news of any one of her children being sick or passing on. Once she told me that I was a star and I never forgot it. It was done so "matter of fact" that I embraced it, knowing that is how she viewed me. It took me years to recognize that the light she saw in me was what I needed to discover and start shining. In retrospect, even her sense of fashion and style has become a part of who I am today; her clothing identified how she operated, from the housewife to the woman going out to tend to business affairs, to the lady who was stepping out to church. She rubbed off on me! I have followed in her footsteps to dress up with classical simplicity that identifies with all of life that I participate in.

Although she was old and certainly ready to go, I cried at the news of her passing because of the symbolism of a few nights before. While I was on vacation in Dominica, I saw a fading star, and I was explaining to my friends that its life span was over, and the blinking symbolized it was dying. Then I found out Adelaide was gone within the same timeframe as that star. She had risen up early that October morning, and she told her caregiver that all was well, and she went back to sleep for the final time, at peace and full rest.

My life guides, who showed up as my grandmother and great-grandmother, were assisting me in lessons that I am now able to confidently embrace. I have come to a place in my life where I can honestly check on my feelings and respect what has come to visit me for a while. I am able to sit with them for a moment, and I have become quite skillful and able to recognize and call my visitors by name: this one is doubt (makes me question my every move and even my self-worth); this one is fear (there is a monster under the bed and in the closet and no matter what you do, he is going to get you, and you will never win); this one is lack of forgiveness (I hope they fall into the pit of no return); this is bitterness (the very thought of it brings bile in my mouth), and yes, this is malice (I have something against you and I will not let it go). Yes, I am calling a spade a spade.

Saying goodbye, adios, and sayonara to these visitors became very necessary for me to begin to focus on having a highly productive life. All those visitors mentioned above brought me to a place of imprisonment, which carried invisible shackles that were turning me into a small, petty-minded, non-progressive person. It became very necessary to understand what was causing my delay, so I began to function on a high level so I could operate and create successful days for my life.

Now I learn to embrace visitors that keep me alert and challenge me to grow: peace brings tranquility to my very soul, and I can sing and declare every little thing is going to be alright; joy comes in the butterflies of excitement that makes me want to dish it out and share some with everyone; love strolls around reminding me that this makes all the difference in the world, just remain calm; then boldness makes an appearance and gives me eagle's wings to SOAR and BE who I am called to become!

Both good and bad visitors come to first label you and then own you with their names. If you own bitterness, then you will be renamed as bitter, and if you own joy, then you will be renamed as joyful.

Yes. Yes. Yes. I now do my best to stop the bad ones at the door and let them make their exit as quickly as hot coal from my bosom. Yes. Yes. Yes. I entertain the good ones and invite them in to sit and dine with me for as long as possible!

Claiming The Me I Discovered

I laugh out loud.
I love to eat.
I love to sleep and be lazy at times.
I love drinking coffee in the mornings.
I love my friends.
I can be impatient.
I like being warm.
Camping for me involves a bed.

Swimming – learning to float.
I love creative projects.
I can play anything.
I like to make a lot of noise, but then nothing comes of it.
I am deeply introspective, but no one learns from me.
I pursue my best physical self, yet I refuse to drink water and eat a properly balanced nutritional meal.

And how have you grown?

I am fiercely loyal in what I believe.
I love my family, even when we are at odds.
I love falling asleep with a good book; I love opening a good book no matter how tired I am.
I have a whole new discovery to make about myself.
I can be a better person.

I am always challenging myself to do new things, for example, riding a bike, starting a business, etc.

If you strongly desire to grow and excel in any area of your life, never allow comfort to become your friend. Comfort, in any area of your life where you need to grow, is not your friend. You must be determined to transform by creating new habits and behaviors that will assist you in shaping your creativity, giving, and success that will foster persistence in taking the necessary steps for you to grow. Embracing comfort on any level is to tell yourself that you are now fully satisfied and content, but you can end up settling for less when you are choosing not to stand up to your full potential. If we are not mindful, old habits called comfort can creep in and present a false sense of tranquility to free you from pushing to better.

There is a level of persistence that needs to become a part of the day-to-day you. Become focused to see every detail completed. **Work a plan to get it done.** You can successfully follow through and complete each task by getting the challenging ones out of the way quickly, or you can look at each task making excuses and formulating reasons why it must be placed in a holding pattern. This will cause you to create further delay in your day becoming successful and even hinder you from moving on to something that can be progressive and meaningful in life.

Challenge yourself to get to the greener side:

- I get excited walking along this journey called life. I am being challenged to walk another path that is not conventional.
- Discover a different route driving home.
- Walk up the stairs instead of riding the escalators.
- Do the hundred-meter dash with a three-year-old who keeps telling you to go faster.
- Sing and dance on top of your lungs with pre-teens who surprise you with their musical voice range.
- Look at life day by day and employ the urge to appreciate the moments and what can be accomplished in them.
- Depend or be dependent on someone with the knowledge and or understanding that no one walks this earth alone,

but you can only discover who you are with others around you.
- People mirror what they see in you. You smile, they smile.

For you created my inmost being; you knit me together in my mother's womb. I praise you because I am fearfully and wonderfully made; your works are wonderful, I know that full well. My frame was not hidden from you when I was made in the secret place, when I was woven together in the depths of the earth. Your eyes saw my unformed body; all the days ordained for me were written in your book before one of them came to be. How precious to me are your thoughts, God! How vast is the sum of them! Were I to count them, they would outnumber the grains of sand—when I awake, I am still with you. (Psalm 139:13-18 - NKJV).

This scripture assures us that no matter what our circumstances are, we were never a mistake. It also serves as a reminder that we were always a part of God's plan. Your skin tone, eyes, lips, limbs, the sound of your voice, and your family are a construct of how you were shaped to enter into this game of life. Therefore, it becomes a responsibility for you to grasp who you are and develop a desire to share the best of you to others so they can also embrace the uniqueness that is built from the very inside. Oh, how marvelous are the thoughts that brought you here. Memorable moments will come from your smile, walk, conversations, and personality that no one else can provide.

Free To Be

You are qualified to embrace, express yourself, and share with others the simple joy of being you without apology or permission. Gaining freedom to express oneself means to recognize both your weaknesses and strengths, as well as being comfortable in the acknowledgment of them all. To become comfortable in your skin is to become silent and observe your past experiences and look at how you represented yourself on these occasions. You will begin to get pointers on how you handle stress, unpleasant encounters, and compliments. These factors will begin to bring enlightenment to show you how you are representing yourself. You are presented with these observations to decide if you are being true to yourself and also if you are comfortable in the way you handle yourself.

Get rid of the load of negativity, and you will begin to see the possibilities of your whole life. Sometimes it will come full blast, and sometimes, it enters like a spark. Getting to own you becomes even more rewarding when you are able to gain control of your feelings. The main thing about living the best you is discovering that what you are already giving to the world is truly the best you have to offer. There are always new areas to establish that will continue to push through once you begin to be your true authentic self. Like attracts like; therefore, the people who surround us are a reflection of who we are. No one entertains what they dislike, so we are always "comfortable" with what we recognize, and the marvelous thing about embracing changes in yourself is the endless possibilities of what is ahead of you.

Falling down and getting back up to make a new discovery about self can be terrifying and exhilarating at the same time. It is really taking the first exploration, asking, "What else can I do with my life?" Remember, you only fail when you refuse to get up after falling down.

Own you! Whether good or bad, whatever may come your way, you must be your best. Placing blame on others cannot be your portion; always check who you are and where you are. Questions will arise to challenge you, including the ones you ask yourself, and you are the only one who will know without fail whether you fell behind or held your standard. In growing up to own you, the learning curve provides a scale to who you are and where you are striving to go. You must not turn a blind eye or try to lower the scale to your liking. Once your focus is upwards, no matter the setback, you will make progress even if nothing seems to be happening.

You must trust the process in the areas of newness for growth to take place. It takes time for trees to grow, and it takes a specified time for babies to develop. The bigger your expectation for growth, is the more time and involvement this process of building you will take to manifest.

For he will be like a tree planted by the waters, which spreads out its roots by the river, And will not fear when the heat comes; But its leaf will be green, And will not be anxious in a year of drought Nor cease to yield fruit. (Jeremiah 17:8 - NJKV).

This scripture comes with such reassurance that as long as you are striving and focused in the right direction, then you cannot fail. We must never have an illusion that our life comes without obstacles. There are going to be periods of setbacks that will cause doubt if you are not prepared for the obstacles that might arise. There has never been a promise of comfort and ease but of faith and works that will yield results. It is through the adversities our growth shows up, and we are not the only one who becomes aware of it, but others will come to recognize it as well. Therefore, your character will show up and represent you at all times. Sit up and pay attention to yourself, and have the courage to see what others see at times.

"Owning you" means I have my up and my down days, and whichever day you are greeted with, it becomes vital to strive for a better or greater you no matter what!

Some days we must admit, "I was not my best self today; my best-self did not show up on this matter." However, you must give yourself the opportunity to go again without being mired in guilt.

The table we are invited to sit at will show us our company. Our company has its own characteristics and can be identified as being progressive, bold, steadfast, successful, powerful, graceful, joyous, fun-loving, destructive, and defeated. A reflection of who you are and where you are going will enhance the company. If you are a builder, baker, designer, singer, or teacher, then you will be pulled in that direction once you begin to recognize the key in owning who you are and what you will do about yourself.

Ask yourself, "Where do I need to go? Who do I need to become daily?"

Seek out the paths that will demand and create a transformed you.

Knock on the door of your heart to be opened to the treasure that is you.

Chapter 8

Ask, Seek, Knock

I have been using these three action words throughout our conversations based on a revelation of how important they are in our everyday life.

Making this a lifestyle will enable you to be at a continuous place of enquiring, learning, and encountering new things. If you have the mindset that all good things come to those who wait, then you must already know what you are waiting on to come to past. All your desires, great or small, must be placed on the action wheel.

Ask and it will be given unto you; seek and you will find, knock and the door will be opened unto you. For everyone who asks receives; the one who seeks finds; and to the one who knocks, the door will be opened. (Matthew 7:7-8 - NKJV).

The Bible is written as a guide and filled with prosperous instructions for our lives. The principles apply to our spiritual well-being as well as the physical domain in which we operate so that all channels and avenues become available to bless us. The scriptures also remind us that our Father in heaven knows before we ask what we already need. However, in order for Him to operate, we must come in alignment and into a relationship with Him, so He can operate legally in our lives. The only way to do this is to invite God into our lives and give all the matters that concern us to Him.

Engage yourself in your expectation for your best life.

If you then, though you are evil know how to give good gifts to your children, how much more will your Father in heaven give good gifts to those who ask him! (Matthew 7:11 – NKJV).

Therefore I tell you, whatever you ask for in prayer, believe that you have received it, and it will be yours. (Mark 11:24 – NKJV).

But let him ask in faith, nothing wavering. For he that wavers is like a wave of the sea, driven and tossed by the wind. (James 1:6 – NKJV).

You build courage, boldness, and faith when you ask for the things concerning you. It is not only to the Lord but unto man who you must ask for a raise, loan, among other things.

So, when you pray, ask and do not doubt, and you will receive.

Seeking is an earnest desire to go after what you want. Seeking is an attempt to find or a desire to obtain or achieve.

There are conditions to be met in order for you to be rewarded. What are you seeking after in this time and season of your life?

If you need to be educated, then you go seeking after the process to become educated.

If you want to be a successful entrepreneur, go seeking after those who have successfully completed the process and see the model that worked for them.

If you want to become a prayer warrior, seek out the things of the kingdom of God and enquire of those who have experienced miraculous breakthroughs in their prayer life.

Whatever it is you so desire, begin to seek and go after it, and what you seek after will find you in simple, amazing, and unlikely ways.

When you are seeking, you begin to think and talk about it, and you also begin to speak those things that are not there as though they are. Use your imagination to really see and take a hold of what you seek and never quit until you get a hold of it.

We must be careful that we are not too narrow-minded that we miss our blessings because we are expecting it to come only in a specific way and from a specific person. Seeking is a promise from God that if you spend the time to do it, you will be rewarded.

You will seek me and you will find me when you search for me with all your heart. (Jeremiah 29:13 - NKJV).

I sought the Lord and he answered me; he delivered me from all my fears. Those who look to him are radiant; their faces are never covered with shame. (Psalm 34:4-5 - NKJV).

Indeed if you call out for insight and cry aloud for understanding, and if you look for it as for silver and search for it as for hidden treasure, then you will understand the fear of the Lord and find knowledge of God. For the Lord gives wisdom; from his mouth comes knowledge and understanding. (Proverbs 2:3-6 - NKJV)

We can look to acquire tangible things in a certain time because there are scales built to determine when specific skills can be acquired in order to consider ourselves knowledgeable, such as a diploma or degree. Conditions are set in place that if we fulfill set requirements, then we can achieve recognition and rewards based on what we have accomplished.

To knock is to attract attention to gain entry. This is to move boldly and encourage yourself to go after what you want.

And behold, a woman of Canaan came out of the same coasts, and cried unto him, Saying, Have mercy on me, O Lord, thou Son of David, my daughter is grievously vexed with a devil. But he answered her not a word. And his disciples came and besought him, saying, Send her away; for she cries after us. But he answered and said, it is not meet to take the children's bread and to cast it to dogs. And she said, Truth Lord, yet the dogs eat of the crumbs which fall from their master's table. Then Jesus answered and said unto her, O woman, great is thy faith, be it unto thee even as thou wilt. And her daughter was made whole from that very hour. (NKJV).

There was in a city a judge which neither feared God nor regarded man. And there was a certain widow in that city and she came unto him saying, Avenge me of mine adversary. And he would not for a while, but afterward he said within himself, thought I fear not God nor regard man; Yet because the widow troubleth me, I will avenge her, lest by her continual coming she weary me. (Luke 18: 2-5 – KJV).

Knocking is an earnest desire to go after what you want. Knocking is to become persistent in getting your desired results. The woman kept on coming with her plea – "Grant me justice against my adversary." For some time, the judge refused. But finally he said to himself, Even though I do not fear God or care what people think, because this widow keeps bothering me, I will see that she gets justice so that she will stop bothering me.

When you know what you want and know that it is yours to get no matter the opposition, then you have to become persistent in knocking and pressing no matter who it annoys.

We can become mortified by the way we are treated, but both women knew that someone else had what they needed in order to rejoice victoriously.

Free To Be

The one thing we cannot regain is time, and once we understand this precious commodity that marks our history, we shall aspire to use it as best as we can.

There is something for you to accomplish daily when you choose for your life to become highly productive. It is, in essence, the beauty of what unfolds that we discover our effectiveness in what we choose to do and pursue.

Become consistent and persistent in whom you choose to develop and become. As you have discovered, life takes work, and it requires you to show up and participate in how you are going to take the day. The best way to operate is to size yourself up and see where you already are and where you need to go next. Does it require asking, seeking, or knocking; one or all?

Say it out loud and make a declaration by first speaking to the Lord: "I see this... I need help here..." and look at where He shows you to go, what you need to seek after, and who should assist in unlocking doors for you to enter.

Everything begins with the first step, and when you take that step, it assures you that you can take another step. In taking these habitual steps, you begin to walk, and it is necessary for you to be engaged in this same process continuously in order to experience timely blessings in your life.

When you come to a fork in the road, you must enquire about any checkpoints you might be missing.

Ask: It is a requirement for heaven to hear your request.

Seek out the treasures; they are waiting to be located.

Knock so you can enter through the door of all possibilities.

About the Author

Maureen Thomas is a well-rounded speaker and motivator. She has a Bachelor of Science degree, matriculating in Sociology and Psychology. Maureen is a member of Christ Theological Consortium and affiliated with Christ Theological Seminary and has received the honor of Plenary Academician of the Consortium. Publicly, Maureen has been recognized for her leadership and contributions to development, teaching, inspiration, and encouragement. Through the birth of her Women's Ministry, Maureen is also the creator of her Women's Conference: "Broken to Be Blessed!" Her ministry has ignited the spark to speak to men and women across the nations.

Currently, Maureen is the pastor of Jerusalem A Church Without Walls and also the dean of Jerusalem School of Ministry, where she also instructs. The *Living Today With Pastor Maureen* show is one of her current creations, which can be viewed on various social media platforms, addressing issues of life.

CPSIA information can be obtained
at www.ICGtesting.com
Printed in the USA
BVHW071212100521
606942BV00005B/676